DIVING AND SNORKELING GUIDE TO

Bonaire
and **Curaçao**
including
information on **Aruba**

by George S. Lewbel, Ph.D.,
and the editors of Pisces Books

🌀 **Pisces Books** ● New York

ACKNOWLEDGMENTS

The author very much appreciates the assistance of Mr. Elio Romjin and Mr. Eitel Hernandez of the Curacao Tourist Bureau; ALM Antillean Airlines; Dr. Tom van't Hof and Dr. Jeff Sybesma of the Netherlands Antilles National Parks Foundation (STINAPA) and the Curacao Underwater Park; Mr. Oswaldo Serberie and Mr. Erold Martina of Dive Curacao & Watersports; Mr. van der Horst of the Princess Beach Hotel; Mr. Frank Engelhardt of Masterdive Scubashop; and Mr. Ben van Dalen of Piscadera Watersports.

Also, Luis De Palm of the Bonaire Tourist Bureau in Kralendijk; Don Stewart, Frank Fennel, Morey Ruza, and Dave Serlin of Captain Don's Aquaventure Habitat; Dee Scarr of Touch the Sea; David Feinberg of the Flamingo Beach Hotel; and the Hotel Bonaire.

Publishers Note: At the time of publication of this book, all the information was determined to be as accurate as possible. However, when you use this guide, new construction may have changed land reference points, weather may have altered reef configurations, and some businesses may no longer be functioning. Your assistance in keeping future editions up-to-date will be greatly appreciated.

Also, please pay particular attention to the diver rating system in this book. Know your limits!

Library of Congress Cataloging in Publication Data

Lewbel, George S.
   Diving and snorkeling guide to Curacao and Bonaire with information on Aruba.

   Bibliography: p.
   1. Skin diving—Antilles, Lesser—Guide-books.   2. Scuba diving—Antilles, Lesser—Guide-books.   3. Curacao—Description and travel—Guide-books.   4. Bonaire—Description and travel—Guide-books.   5. Aruba—Description and travel—Guide-books.   I. Title.
GV840.S782A645   1984   797.2'3'09729
                            84-1179
ISBN 0-86636-035-2

Printed in Hong Kong

10 9 8 7 6 5 4 3 2 1

Staff

Publisher	**Herb Taylor**
Project Director	**Cora Taylor**
Series Editor	**Steve Blount**
Editors	**Carol Denby**
	Linda Weinraub
Assistant Editor	**Teresa Bonoan**
Art Director	**Richard Liu**
Artists	**Charlene Sison**
	Alton Cook
	Dan Kouw

Table of Contents

How to Use this Guide

This guide will acquaint you with a variety of dive sites on Curacao and Bonaire and provide information that you can use to decide whether or not a particular site is appropriate for your abilities and intended dive plan. If you arrive ready to jump in the water, you'll find dive-by-dive descriptions in Chapter 2, Diving on Curacao and Chapter 4, Diving on Bonaire. Read the entire chapter before selecting a site, since some material that is common to several sites is not repeated for each one. Chapter 6, Safety, should be read first, because it covers both routine and emergency procedures.

Sooner or later, you'll have to put in some surface time to get rid of that excess nitrogen you've built up underwater or to let your skin dry out. On early trips to the Netherlands Antilles, I tried to keep that surface interval short because the diving was so good, but looking back on those trips I'd have to admit that I shortchanged myself. The Netherlands Antilles are extremely interesting islands, with spectacular scenery both above and below the water line. Where else in the Caribbean can you find wild parrots nesting in cactus, limestone caves with growing stalactites and crystalline pools, lunar landscapes, and coral reefs, as well as a friendly populace that speaks four languages? Chapter 1, Overview of Curacao, and Chapter 3, Overview of Bonaire, offer descriptions of the islands' history, geography, scenery, and some general information on accommodations, services other than diving, and shopping. Appendix I is a selected list of hotels, dive shops, and dive operators, and will be helpful to you if you need to make your own hotel and diving arrangements on arrival.

Wall diving and sponges are almost synonymous with the "ABC" islands of the Netherlands Antilles. Photo: L. Martin. ▶

The Rating System for Divers and Dives

A conventional rating system (novice, intermediate, advanced) is really not practical on a site-by-site basis for most locations on Bonaire and Curacao. Both islands have fringing reefs that start on a shelf or submarine terrace near shore, curl over a lip at depths ranging from 20 to 40 feet (6–12 meters) and then continue down a dropoff. Nearly every site therefore includes good shallow-water diving on the terrace and on deeper areas over the lip; a description of typical dive depth would be meaningless for most sites.

We do have some recommendations as to which parts of the typical reef profile are suitable for divers of various skill levels, though. Inexperienced divers should never place themselves in any situation where loss of buoyancy control could result in rapid depth increases. This translates as advice to keep away from walls (that is, near-vertical or vertical dropoffs). Diving on or near walls is considered safe only for advanced divers, or for intermediate divers under proper supervision. Gradual dropoffs present less hazard, and diving on or below the lip of these dropoffs (slopes less steep than 45°) is considered safe for well-supervised novices. The word *supervised* should be understood to mean that a diver is under the direct supervision of a qualified instructor or divemaster.

Few divers know that the wreck of the La Machaca *was originally in 120 feet of water. Diving on it had to be carefully planned. Photo: H. Taylor.*

These recommendations should be taken in a conservative sense, keeping in mind the old adage about there being old divers and bold divers but few old bold divers. It is assumed that any diver using this guide is in decent physical condition. A *novice* diver is defined as a diver who has recently completed a basic certification sport diving course, or a certified sport diver who has not been diving recently or who has no experience in similar waters. An *intermediate* diver is defined as a certified sport diver who has been diving actively for at least a year following a basic course, and who has been diving recently in similar waters. An *advanced* diver is defined as someone who has completed an advanced certification sport diving course, and who has been diving recently in similar waters.

You will have to decide yourself, of course, if you are capable of making any particular dive depending on your level of training, recency of experience, physical condition, and on the water conditions at the site. Remember that water conditions can change at any time, even during a dive. Penetration of wrecks, diving in caverns or caves, or diving below a depth of 100 feet (30 meters) is considered to be suitable only for advanced divers with specialized training in these skills. Diving below a depth of 130 feet (40 meters) is considered to be outside the realm of sport diving.

Now in 35 feet of water, La Machaca is a dive that most divers can enjoy easily, and safely. Photo: L. Martin.

1

Overview of Curacao

Curacao Island (pronounced cur-ah-sow) is the largest of the six Netherlands Antilles islands. The Netherlands Antilles include the three "ABC" islands—Aruba, Bonaire, and Curacao—which lie within sight of Venezuela, and three smaller islands, St. Maarten, Saba, and St. Eustatius, 600 miles (960 kilometers) to the north. Curacao is 38 miles (60 kilometers) long and 7 miles (11 kilometers) wide, and its capital, Willemstad, is the seat of government for the six islands and the largest town in the islands.

Curacao has been politically, economically, and militarily valuable for over four hundred years despite its virtual lack of most natural resources. It has been important primarily because it has a large protected harbor where large warships can be anchored and guarded. This anchorage (St. Anna Bay) has been in demand since the early sixteenth century. When other countries squabbled for supremacy on the high seas, control of Curacao's harbor was one of the keys to power in the Caribbean. Curacao's history is therefore more complex than you might expect for such a seemingly remote island. Indeed, Curacao's present-day diversity is the happy end-product of that complicated history.

Before their discovery by Europeans, the islands were inhabited by the Caiquetios, a tribe of Arawak Indians. Their traces remain in the form of pictographs painted with red dye in various caves. The islands were discovered in 1499 by a Spanish expedition whose navigator was Amerigo Vespucci, for whom America was named. The ABC islands were claimed by the Spanish from their discovery in 1499 until 1634, although the Spanish initially considered the islands useless because they lacked precious metals. Unfortunately, the Spanish did not feel the same about the Caiquetios, and deported all but a handful of the 2,000 inhabitants to work in the copper mines in Santo Domingo. The Spanish then converted Curacao into a ranching island by bringing in cattle and sheep. Curacao was also used as a port by slavers who captured mainland Indians.

Being isolated in the south central Caribbean, the Netherlands Antilles offer a diversity of marine life that matches the best Caribbean locations. ▶

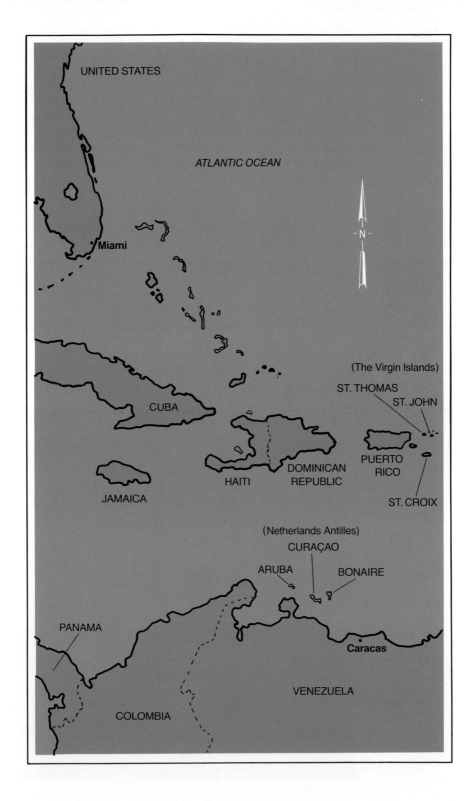

UNITED STATES

ATLANTIC OCEAN

-N-

Miami

(The Virgin Islands)

ST. THOMAS

ST. JOHN

CUBA

PUERTO
RICO

DOMINICAN
REPUBLIC

ST. CROIX

HAITI

JAMAICA

(Netherlands Antilles)

CURAÇAO

ARUBA

BONAIRE

PANAMA

Caracas

VENEZUELA

COLOMBIA

Spanish colonial rule on Curacao ended in 1634 when the Dutch, involved in a war with Spain, took the island. Over the next two centuries, the Dutch built four forts—Fort Amsterdam, Waterfort, Riffort, and Fort Nassau—to protect St. Anna Bay. When the war ended in 1648, the ABC islands remained Dutch colonies.

The Dutch became heavily involved in the black slave trade during the seventeenth century. Curacao was used as a major stopover and transhipment location by slavers from Africa, whose human cargo was allowed to rest and regain some strength after the brutal Atlantic crossing. Elegant plantation houses (*landhuizen*) were constructed as status symbols and staffed with slaves, although it was all but impossible to raise most crops on the arid land. Some of these landhuizen have been preserved as historical monuments and can be visited today by tourists. The slave trade continued to flourish on the island until the mid-eighteenth century, and was not officially abolished until 1864.

Despite their acceptance of slavery, the Dutch were tolerant of differing religious and political views. The Netherlands Antilles sheltered refugees from all over the world. Many Jews, fleeing religious persecution during the eighteenth century, emigrated to Curacao from the Netherlands and from Brazil. The Brazilian Jews spoke Portuguese, as did the coastal slave traders. Traces of this heritage can be found in one of the island

The modern and the antique come together in the harbor at Willemstad on Curacao. The red roofs of traditional Dutch buildings contrast with waterfront highrises.
Photo: L. Martin.

languages, Papiamento (also spelled Papiamentu)—a Portuguese-based mixture that includes some Spanish, Dutch, English, and African words. There is still a large Jewish population on Curacao, and Mikve Israel Synagogue is the oldest synagogue in the western hemisphere. The Dutch Catholic church sent missionaries to convert African slaves to Christianity, and evidence of their work is still present; most of Curacao's residents are Catholic.

The modern period for Curacao began with the arrival of the oil industry. Due (once again) to the need for a safe harbor, Royal Dutch Shell built a refinery in 1915 in St. Anna Bay to process and store oil from Venezuela. Modernization and industrialization soon followed. Shell Curacao was the single largest employer on the island for many years. When World War II broke out, the Shell refinery became a crucial link in the supply of petroleum to the Allies, and Curacao drew closer economically to the United States.

The Netherlands Antilles were granted independence from the Kingdom of the Netherlands in 1954. Each of the ABC islands and the other three islands (called the Windward Islands as a group) have separate governments, and there is a single parliament (*de Staten*) which handles issues affecting all of the islands.

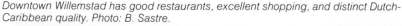

Downtown Willemstad has good restaurants, excellent shopping, and distinct Dutch-Caribbean quality. Photo: B. Sastre.

Curacao Island Today

If you're the same way I am about diving, you probably hope to spend the maximum amount of time underwater with the minimum surface interval before getting back in again. Fortunately, if you're doing any shore diving you'll have to drive through the Curacao countryside to get to the good spots. It's worth the time—even if you miss a morning's dive—to roam around the island by car. Curacao is completely different from the usual lush Caribbean island many visitors expect. It has large sections of extremely rugged desert terrain, small rural villages, and a surprisingly sophisticated modern city, Willemstad, with a population of over 165,000.

Curacao is a dry, hilly island. It has volcanic baserock which is capped in most places by limestone, the remains of ancient coral reefs. This limestone is continually being slowly dissolved and eroded. The process of dissolution results in many underground caves and caverns. Above ground and along the shore, erosion leaves limestone with very sharp edges. At the beach, eroded limestone is referred to as "ironshore," and you'll need booties and gloves to get over it safely where there isn't any sand.

Although there are palm trees here and there and orchids grow on the sides of some of the higher hills, most of the natural vegetation is cactus and thorn bushes. You've probably seen various extracts of aloe vera for sale as a soothing skin lotion or remedy for sunburn; the aloe plant from which the sap is extracted grows all over Curacao, and was once raised there on large plantations. The plants look like yuccas with thick, long, pointed green leaves.

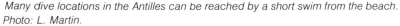

Many dive locations in the Antilles can be reached by a short swim from the beach. Photo: L. Martin.

Paperwork. A word to the wise about documentation and international travel is included here. To get into the Netherlands Antilles from the United States, you'll need some proof of citizenship such as a birth certificate, passport, or voter's registration card, and a return ticket. You'll then be issued a temporary visa card, which you'll have to surrender to get out of the country. If you're bringing minors along, and both parents aren't accompanying the minor(s), bring a notarized letter from the absent parent giving you permission to take the child to the Netherlands Antilles for a vacation. When you leave the Netherlands Antilles, there is a tax (about $6 US in early 1984) at the airport, so save some money for your departure.

Climate. The climate in the Netherlands Antilles is extremely predictable: windy and warm, or very windy and warm. The islands lie beneath the trade winds, which blow from the east 24 hours a day, year-round. The weather is best for diving in the summer and fall. During the first half of the year, especially from January through April, wind velocities are highest and water roughest in unprotected locations. This is a consideration for divers bound for Curacao rather than for Bonaire.

Humidity is low compared to most tropical places—hence the desert vegetation. Average daytime temperatures are in the mid-eighties (about 30°C), but the constant breeze will keep you cool in most locations. Occasional rainshowers are most common in the afternoons, but annual rainfall in the islands is only about 22 inches (55 cm). It's rarely cold enough in the evening to require anything but a light wrap or long-sleeved shirt. The climate is one of the finest in the Caribbean. Daytime as well as nighttime dress on both Curacao and Bonaire is casual.

ALM Airlines is the official airline of the Netherlands Antilles. It operates both between-island service in small propeller planes, such as this, and service via passenger jets to points in the U.S. and other countries. Photo: H. Taylor.

Foreign Exchange. The unit of currency in the Netherlands Antilles is the guilder, abbreviated Naf., which is further divided into 100 cents. As of early 1984, $1 US was worth about 1.7 to 1.8 guilders, depending on where you exchanged your money. American dollars are accepted nearly everywhere, though the exchange rate you're offered at hotels, restaurants, or stores may be a few cents less than at the bank.

Credit cards such as American Express, Mastercard, and Visa are accepted by most businesses, but there can be a few surprises for Americans using their credit cards in the Netherlands Antilles. You are probably aware that the company that issued your credit card also charges merchants about 3%–4% of the total bill when you use it. It's not uncommon for businesses on Curacao and Bonaire to add that percentage to your charges to cover their expenses. If you want to use your credit card to pay your hotel bill, notify the hotel several days before you check out, or you may find that it won't be accepted as you're running for the airport.

Tipping. Tipping in the Netherlands Antilles is similar to tipping in the U.S. The range for excellent service is 10%–15%, with trades relying on tips being those that cater to travelers, such as taxi drivers. Most restaurants add a service charge to your bill as a sort of mandatory tip, so be sure to take a look at the charges before you leave any extra cash.

Boats from neighboring islands and South America are commonly seen at the port of Willemstad. Much shopping and bartering is done right at dockside. Photo: B. Sastre.

A Caution Regarding Electric and Electronic Devices. Although the electric outlets in hotels on Bonaire and Curacao are supposed to put out between 110 and 130 volts AC, the amount actually supplied varies from 100 volts during periods of heavy use to 140 volts or more when things are quiet. In addition, electricity is supplied at 50 cycles per second, not 60 (as in the States). These differences may not seem very important, but they are.

Electronic devices such as radios may be insensitive to the difference in voltage when the supply is less than 120 volts. Appliances that have motors in them, such as razors and hair dryers, often run more slowly than normal when supplied at 50 cycles. Although they're spinning slower, they overheat because they're being fed at higher voltages.

Be extremely careful about plugging your strobe or flashlight charger into ordinary outlets. Chargers designed for 60 cycles will have a drastically reduced output at 50 cycles, and may take two to four times as long as normal to charge your strobe. Be sure to check your charger frequently to make sure it's not too hot, and if the lights in your room suddenly get brighter, unplug your charger immediately or it may turn into a melted block of plastic. Most of the dive operators have a voltage-limited set of outlets specifically for use with chargers, and you are strongly urged to take advantage of them.

Fresh produce is brought daily to Curacao on small boats from Venezuela. Photo: B. Sastre.

Shopping and Dining on Curacao. Most of the services you will want as a diver are available only in or very near Willemstad. Hotel rooms, restaurants, dive shops, car rental agencies, the Curacao Tourist Board (an excellent source of information on the island), camera stores, and so forth are in the city. The best way to find most of these services is to pick up a copy of *Curacao Holiday*, a newspaper-like publication distributed all over the island for free to tourists.

Willemstad is a bustling city of commerce and industry, dominated by the Shell refinery and associated petroleum storage tanks and related facilities. Built around the old harbor of St. Anna Bay, the city is divided roughly in half by the entrance to the Bay with the two halves linked by bridges. The eastern half, called the Punda, is where most of the historic buildings are located.

English is spoken by nearly everyone. You'll have no difficulty coping with menus, which are usually printed in at least two or three languages in larger restaurants. You will find a good selection of restaurants, with seafood an island specialty. Rijsttafel, an Indonesian specialty consisting of a dozen or more tasty small dishes served on a bed of rice, is served proudly by many restaurants. Restaurants range from simple to haute cuisine. If you're addicted to American fast food, you'll find McDonald's, Pizza Hut, Kentucky Fried Chicken, and other such shops in Willemstad. Jamoca almond fudge junkies can take heart: there are three Baskin-Robbins ice cream stores in Willemstad, too!

Hotels on Curacao. There are at present only two hotels on the island that are so thoroughly committed to diving programs that they have dive shops on the premises: the Curacao Concorde (formerly the Hilton) and the Princess Beach.

There are also scores of small hotels in town, most of which are a great deal less expensive than either the Princess Beach or the Concorde. Many of them are air conditioned and equipped with modern conveniences. You'll have ready access to restaurants and shops, too, in exchange for the atmosphere you miss by not being by the water. If you stay at one of the other hotels in town, you can still use the diving facilities at the Princess Beach or the Concorde or rent tanks from Masterdive (the full-service shop in town). None of the small hotels have dive shops on the premises, though some rent masks and snorkels to tourists.

Transportation on Curacao. On many Caribbean islands a car is not essential because of the nature of dive operators and sites, the difficulty of driving in a foreign country, and the cost. On Curacao, however, you'll miss some of the best beach diving—and the most interesting scenery—in the world if you don't arrange for transportation to the back country. Furthermore, if you arrive during the windy season and can't go boat diving, your only practical means of getting into the water will be to drive out to the protected coves of the northwest side of the island.

For non-diving transportation, there are shuttles from the outlying hotels into Willemstad, though the schedules may not suit you since they are designed mainly for casino-goers rather than divers. There are also many taxis within Willemstad, and they have reasonable prices.

Your valid driver's license from the U.S. will be sufficient for driving a rental car, and any hotel can make the arrangements if you don't have one reserved ahead of your arrival. The major car rental companies (for example, National, Avis, or Budget) do business on Curacao, so you can reserve one before leaving home. Keep in mind that international road signs are used, so if you're not familiar with them, ask the car rental agent to explain them to you before setting out. Don't forget that speed limits are in kilometers per hour. Within towns the speed limit is 40 kph; outside of towns, it's 60 kph unless otherwise posted. Drive on the right-hand side of the road, as in the States, and be careful of one-way roads. There are lots of them.

Worthy of a movie set, the wreck of a small tugboat sits upright on a white sand bottom in less than 20 feet (6 meters) of water off Curacao. Photo: L. Martin.

2

Diving on Curacao

This book describes a number of dive locations on Curacao. Some are accessible only by boat and others are accessible from shore. Although not every dive site has been included, this book should guide you to the highlights of some of the best sites.

The southwest shore is more amenable to diving, and most of the diving takes place on that side of the island. The Curacao Underwater Park stretches eastward from Willemstad, along the eastern end (*Oostpunt*) of the southwest shore. The Park and the eastern end of the southwest shore are exposed to more heavy weather than is the western end (*Westpunt*) of the southwest shore. You are strongly encouraged to buy the Guide to the Curacao Underwater Park, produced by the Netherlands Antilles National Parks Foundation, if you plan to dive in the Park.

This book includes sites in the Park—which can be dived year-round, but is much calmer during fall and early winter—and in the area to the west of Willemstad, which tends to be calm year-round.

Curacao Dropoffs. Much of the diving on Curacao is near gradual dropoffs, but some of the dropoffs are sheer vertical walls. Although most dropoffs begin at a depth of 30–40 feet (9–12 meters), they often extend beyond safe limits for sport diving. Compared to Bonaire, the underwater topography of Curacao is more varied, with many more walls. Nearly all sites have good shallow-water diving inshore of the dropoff.

Except for occasionally rough water on the surface in some areas, there are not likely to be any water conditions requiring special techniques for sport divers at the sites mentioned in this guide. Currents are generally minimal (less than ¼ knot) at most of these sites. The dropoffs in the Curacao Underwater Park may have currents (mostly parallel to shore), but drift diving has not yet come to Curacao. If there's some current at a dive site, either be sure that you can make reasonable progress against it or get out of the water. Live boat techniques are not used at this time on Curacao by the dive-tour operators. Remember to begin your dive against the direction of flow so that you can get back to the boat easily if you tire.

A bright orange basket sponge dominates the sloping dropoff at Piedra di Sombre. Photo: L. Martin. ▶

Curacao is a relatively long, narrow island, and may be thought of conveniently as having two sides: a windward shore facing northeast and a leeward shore facing southwest. The northeast shore is rarely dived by visitors, though a few brave locals have their favorite secret spots there. The water is almost always rough on the northeast side of the island, which takes the full brunt of waves driven more or less continually by the tradewinds. Seen from the air, the northeast shore is often white with breaking waves. Sites on the northeast shore are not included in this guide due to difficulty of access and typically dangerous water conditions.

Booties and gloves are strongly recommended for all shore dives. Ironshore can shred your feet and hands. For shore dives, be sure not to swim farther than your capabilities allow for a safe, easy return. For shore diving in particular, novices should be sure that another diver with advanced training is present to help evaluate water conditions. You'll probably not be able to get an independent opinion from a local diver about water conditions, and will have to rely on what you see yourself. You should also take along a dive flag on a float. Before your dive, arrange with someone on shore to keep watch and to meet you at your exit point at a given time. That way, if you have problems, help can be summoned promptly. Be sure to lock your valuables securely in your car, too.

Curacao is not presently a diver-oriented island, and diving tourism on Curacao is fairly undeveloped. Before you pack up and demand a refund, consider this: the diving is outstanding—as good as we've seen anywhere in the Caribbean—and it's mostly virgin or near-virgin diving.

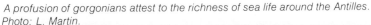

A profusion of gorgonians attest to the richness of sea life around the Antilles. Photo: L. Martin.

Curacao has adequate diving services. You can rent tanks and get good fills; you can rent gear if you don't bring your own; and you can set up complete packages with competent dive operators who can handle your boat or shore needs. You'll just have to do a bit more work to arrange it than you would in a place that is used to 1,000 divers every month, and the water conditions may not be perfect at every location for 365 days a year. Because Curacao is an island, however, there's always a lee side where the diving will be good on almost any day.

Novices Beware. Very few dive guides on Curacao are certified instructors, so if you need training be sure to set it up in advance with the dive operator. Advice from the guides regarding water conditions and the dive site will probably be excellent, but don't count on qualified instruction unless you've arranged for it and have personally verified that your guide is, indeed, an instructor with an internationally recognized certifying agency. Don't be afraid to ask to see a certification card; certified instructors are generally proud to show you where and when they became instructors. You should not plan on taking a certification course on Curacao unless you are accompanied by your own instructor. Curacao thus remains a prime destination for experienced divers, and a less-than-ideal destination for novices unless in a group that includes an instructor.

Air Stations. There is only one air filling station conveniently accessible to visiting divers at the time of this writing (February 1984): Masterdive Scubasports, at Fokkerweg 13, telephone number 54312. Masterdive can arrange for instruction and for car and boat trips to dive sites, and has a very complete selection of diving equipment for sale and rent. Masterdive also can handle some Nikonos repairs and can service a variety of regulators and other equipment. There is an alternative source for diving gear on the island, a smaller shop called Subseas Curacao, at Grenadaweg 10, phone 80271, but this shop has no compressor.

Boat Services. The other two main operators, Piscadera Watersports and Dive Curacao and Watersports, buy air from Masterdive and have full tanks available for rent at their locations in addition to tanks necessary for boat trips. Piscadera Watersports is located on the pier at the Curacao Concorde Hotel, telephone 25000 ext. 177 or 25905. Piscadera operates several boats, including a motor launch and a flat-top, accommodating groups of various sizes. You can also rent diving equipment from them; they have a good assortment of high-quality gear. Their facility is adjacent to showers, pool, beach, restaurant, and other hotel amenities.

The Curacao Concorde is at the mouth of Piscaderabaai (Piscadera Bay), on the west side of Willemstad, and thus has easy access to the relatively protected waters of Blauwbaai, Vaersenbaai, and the other reefs to the northwest of the island.

Dive Sites

Dive Curacao and Watersports is located on the water at the Princess Beach Hotel, telephone 614944 or 82840. Dive Curacao and Watersports also has several boats, including a cabin cruiser and one of the most interesting flat-tops we've ever seen. Customers of Dive Curacao and Watersports can take advantage of a most unusual arrangement that has been made with the Netherlands Antilles National Parks Foundation. Dive Curacao and Watersports packages include regular dives with Dr. Tom van't Hof and Dr. Jeff Sybesma, the two marine biologists responsible for research in the Curacao Underwater Park. Dr. van't Hof is also senior author of the "Guide to the Curacao Underwater Park," and wrote the "Guide to the Bonaire Marine Park." These two biologists are both guides and naturalists, and will provide insights into the Park and its wildlife that you could not get any other way.

The symbol * indicates that the site includes areas that are good for snorkelers and skin divers as well as scuba divers. Many sites are adjacent to dropoffs or walls which extend beyond sport diving depths; where this is the case, the indication of the typical depth range includes the notation *unlimited.*

Dive Site Ratings. Due to the dropoffs and drastic depths a rating chart for most dive sites is not possible. Novice and intermediate divers should be accompanied by a qualified divemaster or instructor when diving. Location names within the Curacao Underwater Park conform to those in the "Guide to the Curacao Underwater Park" by Tom van't Hof and Heleen Cornet; those outside the Park conform to the Shell Road Map of Curacao. Buoy numbers are those used by the Park, which proceed in sequence from west to east end. The dive sites are listed in order of position from Willemstad eastward through the Park, and then from Willemstad westward to Westpunt.

Curacao has had little of the publicity enjoyed by Bonaire and Aruba. Still, its Dutch heritage and underwater sights charm visiting divers. ▶

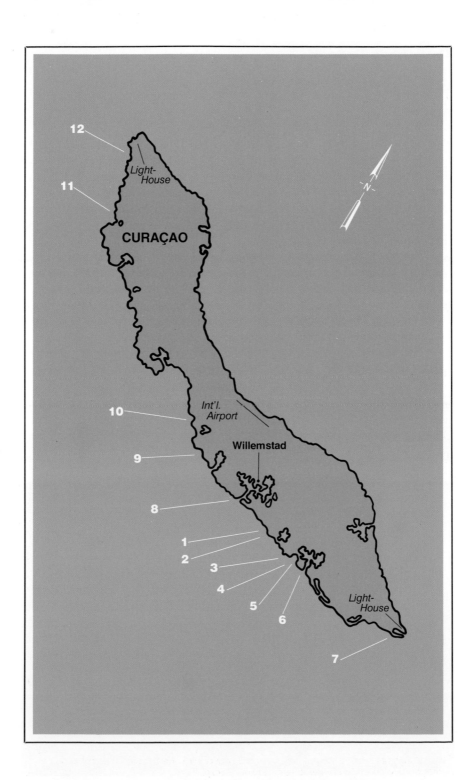

12

Light-
House

11

CURAÇAO

N

10

Int'l.
Airport

Willemstad

9

8

1

2

3

4

5

6

Light-
House

7

23

Oswaldo's Dropoff 1

Typical depth range   :   20 feet (6 meters) to unlimited
Access   :   Shore

The dropoff directly in front of the Princess Beach Hotel is an excellent location for a warmup dive, or for training, or just for the experience of diving on a good dropoff a few minutes' swim from shore. While the shallow shelf inshore of the dropoff might be suitable for novices some of the time, the location is rather exposed and wave action and currents often make this site suitable for novices only when accompanied by a qualified divemaster or instructor.

The shelf has many large heads of elkhorn coral and thickets of staghorn coral and gorgonians. The crest of the dropoff is located at about 40 feet (12 meters). Below this lip, the dropoff slopes downward at about 45° to at least 120 feet (36 meters), where it crests again and then drops more steeply. The dropoff has many heads of brain coral and leaf coral, and is thoroughly covered with sponges.

The easiest entry and exit for this dive is the concrete steps at the mouth of the entrance channel to the Princess Beach Hotel's protected

At the crest of the wall at Oswaldo's Dropoff, a pile of varied coral species attract the usual Caribbean reef crowd: yellowtails, blue chromis and sergeant majors, among others. Photo: L. Martin.

The mounds of coral at Oswaldo's Dropoff are truly impressive, particularly as many are not the common mounding species. Photo: H. Taylor.

anchorage. Dive Curacao and Watersports is the most convenient place to rent tanks for this dive. Be sure to notify the dive shop personnel that you're diving there so they can keep an eye out for you, and stay out of the channel while boats are moving in the area. The dropoff sometimes is washed by currents from left to right as you face seaward, so you should generally begin your dive by swimming offshore and to the left (southeastward) so that you can return downcurrent. Note the alternative exit mentioned for Car Pile, too, in case currents are stronger than expected.

Typical depth range	:	70 feet (21 meters) to unlimited
Access	:	Shore

A large tangled mass of old cars and barges sits on the bottom along most of the coral-covered slope of the dropoff in front of the Princess Beach Hotel. The Car Pile is the remains of an experiment in artificial reef construction that was intended to attract fish as well as divers. The cars are heaped on one another, but many are upright and in pretty good condition, considering their present location! You'll recognize some of your old favorite makes from the 1940s in the pile. If you're careful not to get snagged, you can slip down inside some of the cars on top of the pile for a photograph in the driver's seat. This is an excellent spot for wide-angle shots. Don't get beneath any of the cars or barges, and look out for tangled cables and wire on the bottom. Because of its depth, this dive is recommended for supervised intermediates and more experienced divers only.

A group of car and truck bodies, deposited some years ago, has become a favorite with divers, who swim inside the old wrecks. Photo: L. Martin.

Though the car bodies are now a uniform gray-green, the marine life attached to them, such as these purple tube sponges, is multi-hued. Photo: L. Martin.

For this dive, use the same exit and entry procedure described for Oswaldo's Dropoff. The best way to get to the site is to swim offshore at an angle of about 45° to the right (westward) until you're over the lip of the dropoff. The lip is at about 40 feet (12 meters). Descend on the lip and continue downward to about 70 feet (21 meters), and then proceed farther to the right until you start to see cars. The cars begin at a depth of about 60 feet (18 meters) and continue downward in a gigantic mound to about 130 feet (40 meters).

There is sometimes a current running from left to right (facing the sea), parallel to shore. You don't want to get carried past the pile if the current is strong, so swim straight offshore to the lip, descend, and continue to the right (again, facing the sea) along the 70 foot (21 meter) contour to the pile. On your way back, if you don't want to buck the current, you can exit at a sandy beach past the tennis courts at the west end of the Princess Beach Hotel.

Typical depth range	:	20 feet (6 meters) to unlimited
Access	:	Boat or shore

The buoy for Jan Thiel is within sight of Playa Jan Thiel, a beautiful sandy beach at the mouth of Jan Thielbaai. The bay is well protected by a breakwater, making for easy beach entries and exits. In fact, it looks so much like the perfect beach dive site that it has been used in several films. The beach has picnic facilities, bathrooms, and other amenities. Admission is several dollars a head, but the fee is often waived for tourists. You can reach Playa Jan Thiel by the coast road eastward from the Princess Beach Hotel, or by going west where the road from Bottelier to Caracasbaai dead-ends at the coast.

A bristleworm, or fireworm, threads its way through the maze of passages on a head of giant brain coral. Photo: G. Lewbel.

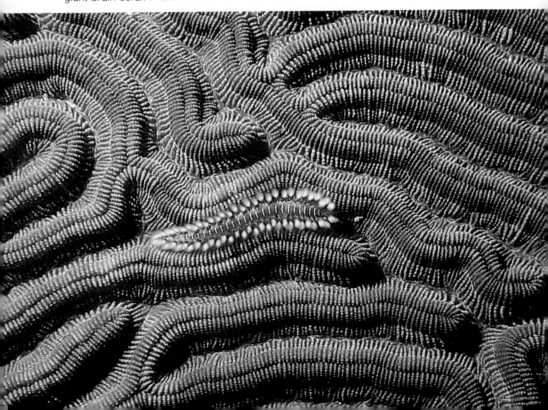

Good for Novices. The bay is mainly shallow sand and turtle grass 10–20 feet (3–6 meters) high in the middle, and thus of interest for training dives. The sides of the bay have some nice coral heads and gorgonian beds along the shore that will tempt snorkelers. There is a coral-covered shelf between the mouth of the bay and the edge of a gentle dropoff just outside the bay. Areas that will be appropriate for novices include the bay itself and the broad, shallow shelf inshore of the dropoff. The gorgonian and coral bed near the mooring is photogenic, and there's a dense thicket of staghorn coral in shallow water.

The dropoff is typical of those within the park, having lots of star coral, gorgonians, sponges, wire coral, and anemones. It falls off at less than 45° in most places, and could thus be an ideal training site for intermediates. Barrel sponges seem more abundant here than at many other nearby dive sites. The lip of the dropoff is within swimming distance of the beach, but if the water is rough or there are currents present, you might have a difficult time once you get outside the breakwater. Currents toward the northwest are not uncommon on and near the dropoff. If you plan to dive the dropoff, a boat is the most convenient way to go.

In the Caribbean, coneys, such as this one, come in a variety of colors and patterns. Photo: G. Lewbel.

Typical depth range	:	20 feet (6 meters) to unlimited
Access	:	Boat

Piedra di Sombré is located between Caracasbaai and Jan Thielbaai. It offers three distinct dives: a stunning vertical wall, a gradual slope, and a shallow terrace. If you plan your dive right, you can see all three areas on a single tank. Facing the sea from the mooring, swim to the edge of the terrace and you'll come to the lip of the wall at a depth of about 30–40 feet (9–12 meters). It is a sheer wall, continuing downward vertically below safe sport diving depths. There are a number of shallow caverns and indentations in the wall, especially in the 70 foot (21 meter) range, where you can see lots of squirrelfish. The wall is covered with wire coral, black coral, star coral, and big sponges.

A large stand of gorgonians and a bed of yellow pencil coral are two of the outstanding features of Piedra di Sombre. Photo: L. Martin.

Just off the dropoff at Piedra di Sombre, gorgonians, or sea whips, cling tenaciously to the coral ramparts.
Photo: L. Martin.

Farther along the wall to the left (facing the sea), the slope becomes less steep and grades into a more gentle slope of about 45°. The slope itself is an excellent dive, having a common crest with the wall and a base that extends below 100 feet (30 meters). It is possible to drop down the wall, track to the southeast on the upward swim, and come up along the slope.

Giant Gorgonians. The shallow inshore area of the terrace around the cement block that anchors the buoy is ideal for snorkeling and underwater photography. It has a large number of anemones in nooks and crannies and a forest of gorgonians. This forest includes some of the largest gorgonians you are likely to see anywhere (one of these monsters is nearly 8 feet tall!).

Typical depth range	:	15 feet (5 meters) to unlimited
Access	:	Boat

This site is outstanding for photography, and offers snorkelers a good look at an intact shipwreck. Towboat (also called Tugboat) is located near the eastern edge of Caracasbaai. The numbered buoy is very near shore, below a collection of petroleum storage tanks and a big orange house on the overlooking cliff. The buoy is somewhat sheltered from prevailing winds, and the site generally is fairly calm. Within a few yards inshore and north of the buoy lies the wreck of a small tugboat, sitting upright on the shelf in less than 20 feet (6 meters) of water. The tugboat is in near-perfect condition, and it is gradually being overgrown with orange tube coral and other animals and plants. If you've used up all your film by

Divers can view this small wreck from the inside out; the wheelhouse portholes make excellent frames for an underwater portrait. Photo: L. Martin.

the time you get to this wreck, you'll probably want to get back on the boat and reload your camera! You'll also want to get one of your fellow divers to serve as a model for portraits in the wheelhouse.

Perhaps the best way to dive this site is not to go to the tug directly, but rather to have a look downslope. To the left of the tug (facing seaward) is a beautiful wall starting at about 30 feet (9 meters). The wall is vertical and even undercut in some locations, and extends downward to depths of about 100 feet (30 meters), below which it takes a more gradual slope of 45° or less. At the base of the wall there are some very large sheet corals. If you swim slightly to your left facing the wall as you return upslope you'll hit the crest of the wall near the tug, and can swim shoreward a few yards to find the wreck.

Boulders of brain coral cling to the gunwales of the tugboat. A steep dropoff nearby hosts stands of wire coral and black coral. Photo: L. Martin.

| **Typical depth range** | : | 20 feet (6 meters) to unlimited |
| **Access** | : | Boat |

Punt'i Piku is just east of Caracasbaai, near the mouth of Spaanse Water (Spanish Water), a large bay used heavily by pleasure boaters. Inshore of the buoy and to the left (facing the sea) is a fine shelf covered with elkhorn and staghorn coral, fire coral, gorgonians, and some very large pillar coral.

Facing seaward, you will find a fairly steep dropoff (over 45°) to the left of the mooring buoy beginning at about 30 feet (9 meters) and continuing to beyond 100 feet (30 meters). The slope is graced by large heads of mountainous star coral at a depth of about 60 feet (18 meters).

If you're after something even steeper, there is a vertical wall on the other side of the buoy, to the right facing seaward. The wall starts at 30–40 feet (9–12 meters) and drops straight down to about 60 feet (18 meters), below which it slopes off more gently. It is covered with wire coral, gorgonians, and sponges.

Lava-like sheets of mountainous star coral drape the edge of the dropoff at Punt'i Piku. Photo: L. Martin.

Barrel sponges, such as these, can sometimes be seen emitting "smoke," a fine mist of particles which, when anchored, will grow new sponges. Photo: L. Martin.

| Typical depth range | : | 20 feet (6 meters) to unlimited |
| Access | : | Boat |

Did you ever find a dive spot so good that you didn't want to tell anyone about it? Well, I did, and I'm going to tell you about it. But there's a catch—you may have to pay some heavy dues to get there, and I don't think the location is likely to be dived very often. Piedra Pretu is located at the eastern end of the Curacao Underwater Park. The nearest harbor is at Dive Curacao and Watersports, about 12 miles (19 kilometers) away. During much of the year, you'll have to ride a boat into heavy chop and high winds for at least an hour before you even see the buoy. Then you'll have to suit up while being bounced around, and you will have another hour's ride home. If you've still got your breakfast in you by the time you get to Buoy #15, however, you're in for a real treat.

While the bright purple tube sponges in the foreground attract attention, the black coral trees silhouetted above the diver are much more rare. Black coral is made into semiprecious jewelry in many parts of the world. Photo: L. Martin.

The black and yellow crinoid on this stand of gorgonians reflexively moves away from an approaching diver. Photo: L. Martin.

Piedra Pretu has the usual shallow terrace above 30 feet (9 meters), suitable for novices. The terrace has staghorn and elkhorn coral and a pretty bed of gorgonians. More experienced divers will want to head for the lip of the wall just to the left (facing seaward) of the mooring buoy. This is one of those spots where you use up all your film in the first five minutes. Piedra Pretu has one of the prettiest vertical walls you're likely to see anywhere in the Caribbean. It runs vertically down to about 120 feet (36 meters), and then slopes off more gradually below that. The wall is covered with a dense forest of black coral. Near the base of the wall, there are big stacked disks of sheet coral the size of table tops. In the 80–90 foot (25–27 meter) depth range, there are crevices going back into the wall, filled with royal grammas and big green moray eels.

Typical depth range	:	90–110 feet (27–34 meters)
Access	:	Boat or shore

The *Superior Producer* is a sunken coastal freighter that rests upright and completely intact on a sand bottom at about 110 feet (34 meters). In 1977, the ship was outward bound from St. Anna Bay, heavily overloaded with a cargo of clothing. After leaving the harbor entrance and turning west, it filled with water and sank within a stone's throw of shore just west of Rif Stadium, the old baseball and soccer field. The top of the wheelhouse is about 80 feet (25 meters) deep, and the bridge is about 90 feet (27 meters) deep, so this dive is for advanced divers only.

The wreck is still fairly clean of marine life, although anemones and corals have started to grow on it. If you want some shots of yourself on the bridge of a large ship, or waving over the railing to the crowds, bring your wide-angle lens and your strobe. The white ceramic toilet in the room next to the bridge suggests some shots, too. There are still some traces of clothing here and there in the large open hold, but local divers got all the really good stuff almost immediately after the ship sank. The cargo and the brass must have been quite valuable; the local divers gave the recompression chamber in Willemstad plenty of business. As I said, it's deep, so be careful to watch your bottom time.

Though a young wreck, the Superior Producer *has attracted a few anemones and other attaching marine organisms. Photo: L. Martin.*

Loaded with clothing when it went down in 1977, the freighter bottomed out at 110 feet (34 meters). Though a deep dive, it's sitting upright on a white sand bottom, making exploration easy. Photo: L. Martin.

You can dive the *Superior Producer* from the shore, although it's better on most days to dive from a boat. The site is exposed to wave action and you'll run a gauntlet of coral heads and urchins all the way to the beach. If you have a very calm day and heavy booties and gloves, you might give it a try. Drive along the shore in front of the old ball park on Gouv. Van Slobbeweg until you come to a big cement block on the beach. The road dead-ends going west; the block is a few hundred yards from the end. You'll then be able to see the mooring buoy for the *Superior Producer* a short distance offshore. Swim to the buoy, head down the cable to the bottom, and then straight out for a short swim to the freighter.

Typical depth range	:	30 feet (9 meters) to unlimited
Access	:	Boat or shore

Blauwbaai (Blue Bay) is a sheltered cove between Piscaderabaai and the town of Dorp Sint Michiel. The bay has a sandy beach, picnic facilities, bathrooms, and a small sundries shop. You'll have no trouble finding it on the Shell map of Curacao. There is a fee of a couple of dollars for entry, but tourists are sometimes exempted from the fee as an act of goodwill. Less than 5 miles (8 kilometers) from Willemstad, it is a popular weekend beach with locals. The bay is also a good spot for a boat dive, offering a protected anchorage and a very pretty dropoff. It's a short run from Blauwbaai to the Piscadera Watersports, the dive operator at the Curacao Concorde Hotel.

If you plan to dive Blauwbaai from the beach, you'll find good snorkeling to either side of the bay entrance along the rocks. The center of the bay is fairly sandy and suitable for training, but not big on scenery. The dropoff at the outer edge of the bay is within swimming distance of the shore, but it's a long way from the sandy beach by the parking lot. Rather than enter

Snorkelers can enter Blauwbaai from the sandy beach, while divers headed for the dropoff find the shore entry near the outside of the bay closer to the wall. Photo: L. Martin.

Yellow pencil coral and brain coral live side by side on the dropoff at Blauwbaai. Photo: L. Martin.

at the sandy beach in the center of the bay if you're going to the dropoff, drive around to the left side of the mouth of the bay (facing the water), just beyond a large pile of concrete rubble and short of a series of very large boulders. The small beach here is within 5 minutes' swim of the lip of the dropoff.

Steep Dropoff. The dropoff at Blauwbaai has a lip at about 30 feet (9 meters) and falls off steeply to depths exceeding 150 feet (46 meters). In some places the dropoff is nearly vertical, but in most areas it is closer to 45°. There are many sheet coral, black coral, wire coral, and sponges on the dropoff. If you're making the transition between diving on slopes and diving on vertical walls, Blauwbaai is an excellent place for training.

Typical depth range	:	30 feet (9 meters) to unlimited
Access	:	Shore or boat

Vaersenbaai is between Dorp Sint Michiel and Bullenbaai, northwest of Willemstad. It can be dived by boat, of course, but the real attraction of Vaersenbaai is that it's an ideal spot for shore training. It is maintained as a weekend retreat for island police officers, and is clean and well kept. There is a concrete parking lot, benches and picnic facilities, and a short pier with steps right into the water. These features make it a popular site with the locals for night diving, too. If you're with a group or class and want a place to gear up without getting sandy, a no-hassle entry and exit, predictably perfect water conditions, and a short swim to a dropoff, Vaersenbaai is right for you. It's about 5 miles (8 kilometers) northwest of Willemstad, on the road to Bullenbaai and Meiberg; just look for the sign to Vaersenbaai on your left.

Vaersanbaai is often used as a site for night diving. It has a parking lot, benches, and the dropoff is a short swim from the pier. Rock beauties, like this one, are often seen at this site. Photo: H. Taylor.

Coral heads and sponge growth on the way to the dropoff may interest divers and snorkelers. Photo: L. Martin.

Vaersenbaai is a protected location and is nearly always calm. It's therefore a good bet when the Curacao Underwater Park is too rough to dive. The dropoff can be seen easily from the beach, since it's only about five minutes' swim away. On the way to the dropoff, there are coral heads that will interest snorkelers. The dropoff is comparable to most of the other dropoffs on the island, cresting at about 30–40 feet (9–12 meters) and sloping downward at about 45° in most places to depths exceeding 100 feet (30 meters).

Typical depth range   :   30 feet (9 meters) to unlimited
Access   :   Shore or boat

Playa Lagun is just south of the town of Lagun, on the coastal road. It has a very small bay and a sandy beach on which fishing boats are usually drawn up. It can be dived by boat but is perfect for a shore dive because of its easy entry and exit, calm water, and nearby dropoff. It is sheltered from weather and remains nearly flat all the time. There is good snorkeling along the base of the cliffs that line both sides of the bay, and a dropoff just a short swim offshore. The dropoff begins at a depth of 30–40 feet (9–12 meters) and slopes downward at about 45° to beyond sport diving range. The center of the bay has a mixture of sand and coral, but the dropoff is fairly solid coral from the lip on down. It's almost a picture-postcard location for training dives. You can drive to within 25 feet (8 meters) of the water, gear up in the shade of trees on the shore, and buy a cold drink from a shop by the beach when you get back out.

A huge, eroded stand of mountainous star coral stands out from the lip of the dropoff. The recesses in such undercut formations often harbor small tropicals such as royal grammas and chromis. Photo: L. Martin.

Open fishing boats, such as these, are in daily use in the Antilles. No boat is needed to dive Play Lagun, however. Good snorkeling is available at the base of the cliffs, and the dropoff is just a short swim away. Photo: L. Martin.

To get there by car, turn off the main road at Dorp Lagun (between Dorp Westpunt and Dorp Soto). The turnoff point is marked by a sign to Playa Lagun. If you're going north, it's a left turn into the parking lot. Another landmark to watch for from the main road is a concrete construction site fenced with barbed wire in the parking lot.

| **Typical depth range** | : | 20 feet (6 meters) to unlimited |
| **Access** | : | Shore or boat |

Playa Kalki is located at the northwestern end of Curacao, and can be reached by boat or by car. If you're in a car, drive to the village called Dorp Westpunt, turn off the main highway at the cemetery, take an immediate left turn at the end of the cemetery, follow the road until you come to a "T," left again a few hundred feet to the head of the concrete stairs, and you're there. You'll find the name of the beach written in coral pieces embedded in the concrete steps leading to the water. It's easier to find than it sounds, and it's well worth the trip. The drive to the tip of the island is beautiful, but the dive offers some really unusual underwater scenery.

Gorgonians line the crest of the dropoff at Playa Kalke. Photo: L. Martin.

A white mist anemone withdraws into a crevice in a star coral boulder.
Photo: L. Martin.

Snorkeling. Playa Kalki is a well-sheltered cove that is calm nearly all the time. You can gear up in the parking lot (be sure to lock your valuables securely), hike down the steps, and dive from the white sand beach. The nearshore coral offers good snorkeling and clear water. Farther offshore, the bottom slopes very gradually downward, in most places at less than 20°. The shallower portions of this area are suitable for novices, since the slope is as gentle as it is on most shelves or terraces above dropoffs in other locations.

The site is also perfect for training, since you can select any depth range you wish and stay within it easily. In most places, there is not really any crest, just a smooth transition from shallow to deeper water. The view downslope from about 30 feet (9 meters) resembles rolling hills seen from a mountain top. Nearly every surface you see is completely covered with living coral. Toward the center of the cove, you'll find compact mounds of star coral forming little Hobbit-like villages at depths of about 60 feet (18 meters). You can also see great piles of sheet or plate coral in deeper water, below 100 feet (30 meters).

3

Overview of Bonaire

Shopping and Dining on Bonaire. The island of Bonaire is largely rural, with only two towns of any size: Rincon, in the interior, and Kralendijk, the island capital. Rincon has very few stores and no services tailored for diving tourists. It does have an excellent home-made ice cream store, however, and a rustic bar that specializes in selling Amstel beer to thirsty visitors to Washington/Slagbaai National Park. Rincon is a very small town, and all roads through town lead past the Amstel bar. Ask anyone in Rincon for directions to the ice cream store. It's hidden up an unmarked side road a couple of blocks from the bar, but it's well worth finding!

Kralendijk has most of the services one would expect in a small town catering to thousands of visitors per year. There is a free newspaper-like publication called *Bonaire Holiday* which contains a city map and advertisements from virtually every hotel, restaurant, store, car rental agency, and dive operator on Bonaire. The center of town covers only a few blocks near the town pier, and you can walk from one end to the other in less than fifteen minutes. All of the services you're likely to need are concentrated there. The main street, J.A. Abraham Boulevard/Breedestraat, has most of the stores along it. There are several large markets, a bakery, and various hardware and sundries stores within a block or two of the main street. Most of these stores (as well as the dive shops at the hotels) sell film and batteries. There are a number of restaurants within a few blocks of the water, and at the major hotels.

On Bonaire, English is spoken by nearly everyone, so you won't have any difficulties with menus or in stores. Water for the island is supplied by a desalination plant, as on Curacao.

An aerial view of Bonaire shows the marked contrast between the parched, desert-like surface and the prolific reefs offshore. Photo: H. Taylor. ▶

Transportation on Bonaire. You won't need a car to go diving on Bonaire, if you're a customer of one of the hotel-based dive operators, but most of their diving will only be between Klein Bonaire and Bonaire. If you want to dive the northwestern end of the island in Washington/Slagbaai National Park, you'll need land transportation; the dive operators typically do not run boats to that end of the island. However, this does not necessarily mean you should rent a car. In the Park, both diving and driving can be challenging, and it's not a bad idea to ask your dive operator to arrange for a van or truck to take you into the park along with an experienced dive guide who knows the area.

Ironically, the Antilles, which have some of the lushest underwater scenery in the world, are semi-arid deserts above water. The contrast between the two environments is fascinating. Photo: B. Sastre

Consider renting a car, though, if only to see the island. Other than within the Park (where some rugged dirt roads may test your aptitude for the Baja 1000), driving is easy on Bonaire. There are several car rental companies in Kralendijk (Avis, Budget, and local companies). You'll need a valid driver's license from the U.S. or another country, as well as some means of establishing your ability to pay for damages (for example, a credit card). Any hotel can make the necessary arrangements for you. Keep in mind that international road signs are used, so if you're not familiar with them, ask the car rental agent to explain them to you before setting out. Don't forget that speed limits are in kilometers per hour. Drive on the right-hand side of the road, as in the States. Lots of roads are one-way, so be careful!

There are lots of taxis within Kralendijk, but they really aren't necessary for most in-town excursions because Kralendijk is so small. The Hotel Bonaire and Captain Don's Habitat are too far from town to walk, though, especially if you have any gear with you. If you're staying there, plan on renting a car or using taxis if you want to spend much time in town.

Salt making, still an important Antilles industry, once dominated the islands' economy. Seawater, let into vast salt pens, was allowed to evaporate, leaving a coating of salt. Slaves, who lived in these tiny huts, raked up and bagged the salt for shipment to Europe. Photo: B. Sastre

4

Diving on Bonaire

As with most islands in the Caribbean, diving on Bonaire can be classified in two ways: diving on the windward side of the island (meaning the side of the island exposed to the constant trade winds) and diving on the leeward side of the island, (the protected side). Though the windward coast offers some spectacular dives, it is usually too rough for some diving most of the year. However, when brief wind shifts occur, usually during September, October, November, or December, the sea on the windward side can be calm. Diving there can be spectacular. Generally, there is less branching coral on the windward side but the marine life tends to be larger. Large grouper and spiny lobsters are much more common on the windward side.

Bonaire is a curved island shaped somewhat like a pork chop. The concave side of the island faces westward, wrapping around a small uninhabited island called Klein (i.e., "little") Bonaire. Klein Bonaire and Bonaire are separated by a channel about one-half mile (.8 kilometers) wide at the nearest point. You can see Klein Bonaire easily from Bonaire. The concave side of Bonaire is the leeward or protected side, since the trade winds blow from the east or northeast. The windward side of Bonaire is seldom dived due to dangerous surf and currents that are driven by the onshore winds. Dives on the windward side of the island are not included in this guide.

The leeward shore of Bonaire has ideal conditions for diving year-round. Virtually all of the diving on the island takes place on the curve of the leeward side as far north as Boca Bartól in Washington/Slagbaai National Park, and around Klein Bonaire. The Bonaire Marine Park includes all waters surrounding Bonaire and Klein Bonaire from the high-tide mark down to a depth of 200 feet (62 meters). You are strongly encouraged to buy a copy of the "Guide to the Bonaire Marine Park," produced by the Netherlands Antilles National Parks Foundation, since all your dives will be within the Park. The Park has about 40 sites permanently marked with buoys on the leeward side of Bonaire and all around Klein Bonaire.

A paradise for divers and snorkelers, Bonaire offers spectacular coral reefs. ▶
Photo: L. Martin.

Gradual dropoffs. On Bonaire and Klein Bonaire, the majority of diving is on or beneath gradual, sloping dropoffs. Walls are not found at most sites on Bonaire or Klein Bonaire. Slopes of 45° or less are more typical. Shallow shelves between the edge of dropoffs and the shore offer excellent snorkeling or diving in the 10–30 foot (3–9 meter) depth range. The water is usually very clear and warm without a thermocline. While you won't sink rapidly out of sight on these slopes, it's easy to get involved in the view and find yourself too deep. At most locations mentioned, the crest of the dropoff is in the 30–40 foot (9–12 meter) depth range, and the coral-covered slope falls off to a white sand bottom at depths of 100–130 feet (30–40 meters).

Currents and Boca Bartól cautions. There are not likely to be any water conditions requiring special techniques on Bonaire or Klein Bonaire for certified sport divers at the sites mentioned in this guide, except for Boca Bartól (which requires knowledge of surf entries and exits). Currents are generally barely perceptible or nonexistent at most sites on Bonaire or Klein Bonaire, again with the exception of Boca Bartól. Boats nearly always anchor at marked buoys and expect you to swim upcurrent to make your dive, returning to the buoy at the end of the dive. For this reason, I recommend against diving from a fixed mooring unless currents are very weak. This will be the case nearly all the time. Keep your eyes and ears open for boats while you're in the water, too. The channel between Bonaire and Klein Bonaire is especially heavily trafficked by dive boats and fishermen.

Booties and gloves are strongly recommended for all shore dives, and the same procedures for shore diving mentioned in Chapter 2, Diving on Curacao, will add to your safety while shore diving on Bonaire. Whether or not you're diving from shore, if you're spending lots of time in the shallows gloves and a full wetsuit will cut your bandage bill way down. The shallows have beautiful thickets of staghorn and elkhorn coral which can cut neat little chunks out of your knees and elbows, and there are large stands of fire coral which look better in photographs than as skin-prints!

Dive Operations

Dive operations on Bonaire are excellent by anyone's standards. Most dive guides on Bonaire are certified instructors or divemasters. They usually dive with hundreds of divers every year, and have a great deal of experience with groups. Additional instruction can be arranged with the dive operators, be it for basic certification or advanced training.

There are three large operators and several smaller ones on Bonaire. The large operators are Captain Don's Habitat, Dive Bonaire (at the Flamingo Beach Hotel), and the Bonaire Scuba Center (at the Hotel Bonaire). The smaller operators include Bruce Bowker's Carib Inn and Buddy Watersports in the center of town. To a large extent, where you stay will probably determine with which operator you dive, since most divers come to Bonaire on a diving-lodging package. If you do have a few extra days not booked with your hotel's dive operator, you are encouraged to try some of the other operators to see how you like them. They all differ from one another in style, but not much in quality—they're all very good.

Captain Don's Habitat. Habitat attracts hard-core divers who consider a tan the sure sign of a non-diver who wasted valuable time on the beach instead of underwater. While novices are welcome here, most of the guests seem to be more experienced. Habitat has an outstanding dive staff, a big air bank with compressors and an endless supply of tanks, rental gear, a complete equipment repair shop, a dark room, several flat-tops, and a fast, open motor launch. Instruction is available at every level from basic scuba to advanced skills. Diving in Washington/Slagbaai Park is also available through Habitat, which can make all the necessary arrangements.

Habitat places a strict limit on the density of divers on each boat, and you'll never be jammed onto an overcrowded boat. When things get busy, additional boat trips are arranged to keep the diving quality high and the load low. Your tank is kept full and accessible 24 hours a day. The reef in front of Habitat is excellent, and a mere two minutes' swim off the pier.

The Bonaire Scuba Center. The Scuba Center, at the Bonaire Beach Hotel has three flat-tops, instructors, a complete shop with compressors and tanks, rental gear, equipment for sale, and a very professional operation. It also boasts a truck outfitted for diving, with rows of seats in the back and equipment racks, so if you're with a group that wants to dive in Washington/Slagbaai Park, this may be the most convenient way to set things up. The Scuba Center can swap boat dives for truck dives if given prior notice.

The location of the Bonaire Scuba Center has been both advantageous and a drawback to its operations. The hotel boasts the only nice sandy beach of the three large hotels, and as such is an excellent spot for training dives. There's a coral reef and a dropoff immediately in front of the dive shop. The beach is also a good place for other water sports (windsurfing, sailing).

Dive Bonaire. Peter Hughes's Dive Bonaire is the shop at the Flamingo Beach Hotel. Dive Bonaire is the largest of the dive operators, and if numbers of happy divers mean success, it is also the most successful. The shop offers qualified instruction; equipment sales, rental, and repair; air and tanks; literally almost anything a visiting diver could possibly want. Its compressor facilities could probably supply the whole island with tanks. Dive Bonaire runs flat-tops and fast motor launches, and specializes in making things easy for diving guests. For example, your tank will be placed on the boat for you, and even geared up if you so desire. All you have to do is put on your rig and fall over the side.

Dive Bonaire is also closely associated with Photo Bonaire, a full-service photo shop capable of developing Ektachrome and other E-6 process films, renting and repairing cameras and strobes, teaching underwater photography classes, and so forth. Photo Bonaire is one of the most comprehensive underwater photography service facilities anywhere.

Undoubtedly part of the success of Dive Bonaire is the appeal of the Flamingo Beach Hotel. It's a more luxurious, comfortable hotel than either Habitat or the Hotel Bonaire, and has several excellent restaurants and shops on the grounds. It attracts its share of hard-core divers, but is also the favored spot on Bonaire for travelers who bring their families to splash in the swimming pool and lie out in lounge chairs in the sun. The Flamingo Beach has managed to fuse a professional dive operation with a semi-luxury hotel, and the combination has very broad appeal.

Dive Sites

The symbol * indicates that the site includes areas that are good for snorkelers as well as scuba divers. Many sites are adjacent to dropoffs or walls which extend beyond sport diving depths; where this is the case, the indication of typical depth range includes the notation *unlimited*.

Dive Site Ratings. Due to the dropoffs and drastic depths a rating chart for most dive sites is not possible. Novice and intermediate divers should be accompanied by a qualified dive master or instructor when diving.

Location names within the Bonaire Marine Park conform to those given in the "Guide to the Bonaire Marine Park" by Tom van't Hof. Buoy numbers are those used by the Park, which proceed in sequence from Lacre Punt at the south end of Bonaire to Kralendijk, circle around Klein Bonaire, then continue to Boca Bartól at the north end of Bonaire. The dive sites in this chapter are listed in approximate order of position from north to south.

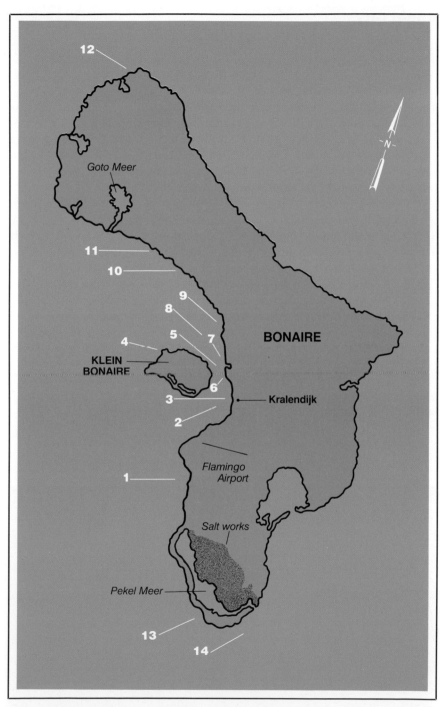

12

Goto Meer

11

10

9

8

7

5

4

KLEIN
BONAIRE

6

3

2

1

BONAIRE

Kralendijk

Flamingo
Airport

Salt works

Pekel Meer

13

14

Most diving on Bonaire is on the southern, concave side of the island, which is in the lee of the prevailing winds. On the windward side, the coral is sparse, though the fish and lobsters tend to be larger.

Typical depth range   :   30 feet (9 meters) to unlimited
Access   :   Boat or shore

The Angel City buoy is located in the center of a series of outstanding dive sites that stretch along two reefs parallel to shore between Punt Vierkant and the pier for the salt works. The buoys for Alice in Wonderland, Angel City, The Lake, and Punt Vierkant are all within sight of one another and are quite similar in topography. Most people favor Angel City because it has large schools of resident fish.

The shelf inshore of Angel City is broad and shallow, and covered with gorgonians, star coral, jumbled piles of staghorn coral, and fire coral. You'll find many nudibranchs among the staghorn coral if you look closely. The shelf nearshore has quite a bit of sand and coral rubble and tends not to be very clear when the water is choppy. Seaward of the buoy, the shelf drops off gently to a pretty sand channel at about 60 feet (18 meters). There are several piles of broken coral that cross the sand channel at right angles; the one at the northern end of the sand channel has one of the largest purple tube sponges you're even likely to see. On the seaward side of the sand channel, the second reef slopes upward to a ridge whose crest is about 40–50 feet (12–15 meters) deep. Between the two reefs, you'll find large numbers of tiger groupers, schoolmasters, and barracudas. The seaward edge of the second reef has a second dropoff that slopes beyond safe sport diving depths.

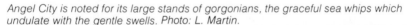

Angel City is noted for its large stands of gorgonians, the graceful sea whips which undulate with the gentle swells. Photo: L. Martin.

A yellowtail poses in front of an enormous colony of tube sponges at Angel City. Photo: L. Martin.

Fish Watching. The most interesting section of Angel City is toward the southern end of the sand channel. If you swim seaward from the buoy till you reach the sand channel and then turn left and go a few hundred feet, you'll come to some big towers of coral. These towers mark the center of a wonderful spot to watch fish. Big schools of black margate swirl around the towers, and there are often horseye jacks and masses of yellow snappers milling about. If you then return to the buoy along the inshore shelf at a depth of about 25 feet (8 meters) you'll pass an enormous mountainous star coral head that has eroded into a small castle, with parapets.

Calabas Reef* 2

Typical depth range : 30–120 feet (9–36 meters)
Access : Shore

Calabas Reef is the area directly in front of Dive Bonaire at the Flamingo Beach Hotel. You can get in and out of the water at the dive shop's pier. All in all, it's a very convenient dive. It's ideal for training, and especially conducive to night diving, due to the lights on the pier and the easy entry and exit.

Once in the water, swim straight offshore to get to the dropoff. There is a stretch of sand and rubble on the shallow shelf. The shelf itself is somewhat barren except for an occasional coral head. Many snorkelers will like it, since there are lots of fish looking for a handout. A short distance farther out, you'll find the crest of the dropoff at about 30–40 feet (9–12 meters), and then a slope that drops downward at about 45° to white sand at over 100 feet (30 meters). The dropoff has good coral off the Dive Bonaire pier, and a small wreck at about 60 feet (18 meters), a bit north of the pier at the opposite end of the hotel complex from Dive Bonaire. There's also an old anchor in about 25 feet (8 meters) of water a little farther north.

It is the peculiar stripes that give the tiger grouper its name, not its generally shy demeanor. Photo: G. Lewbel.

A small ledge purveys a sampler of Caribbean reef growth tube sponges, orange and red encrusting sponge, a gorgonian colony and several species of coral.   Photo: S. Blount.

Typical depth range	:	20–40 feet (6–13 meters)
Access	:	Shore

If you've read any of the dive magazines in the past five years, you've seen pictures taken at Town Pier. It is the ultimate macrophotographer's dive, and the orange tube corals under the pier have appeared in countless posters and travel articles. To see them open, though, you have to dive the pier at night.

Dangers of Pier Diving. There are two piers in town. The Town Pier is the northernmost of the two, located near the end of Simon Bolivar-straat in the center of town next to the fish market. The Town Pier usually has several red and white tugboats and various coastal vessels moored along side. To prevent your being turned into ground round by any of these ships, you may not dive the Town Pier without permission of the Harbormaster, who is responsible for ship traffic near the Town Pier. The Harbor-master's office is in the fort near the Town Pier and is generally open only during the day, so plan ahead. It's also essential to doublecheck with one of the tugboat captains before jumping in the water, since they usually know about last-minute ship schedule changes. Finally, if any vessels are moving in the vicinity of the Town Pier, stay out of the water.

Blackbar soldierfish duck into a crevice . Photo: G. Lewbel.

The polyps of these orange tube corals, seen at night, are extended for feeding. The tiny feather worm is also at work, filtering microscopic food from the warm waters.
Photo: G. Lewbel.

The easiest place to enter and leave the water is the ramp next to the fish market, a small building that looks like a Greek temple across from the end of the pier. The ramp may be slippery, so be careful. Swim directly across the little harbor (staying on the bottom to be safe) to the pier, and try not to use up all your film on the first two pilings you find! You're likely to see big moray eels, orange tube coral, arrow crabs, white anemones, and maybe even some tarpon.

Typical depth range	:	30 feet (9 meters) to unlimited
Access	:	Boat

Carl's Hill is on the far side of Klein Bonaire. The buoy lies between two different kinds of dropoffs, a vertical wall to the east (right, facing seaward) and a more gradual slope of about 45° to the west. It would be difficult to see both areas in a single dive. The site sometimes is swept by currents, thus determining your direction of travel for you. Carl's Hill is well populated with fish, including a number of morays that have been fed routinely by divers.

You can get to the wall by swimming east from the mooring buoy. You'll cross a small buttress and a sand channel before you get there, so don't give up; the swim will probably take you about five minutes. The wall extends downward from about 30 feet (9 meters) to about 70 feet (21 meters), below which it grades smoothly into a sloping dropoff that extends below 120 feet (36 meters) to a sand bottom. The wall is covered with corals, big sponges, wire coral, black coral, and sheet coral near the base. The relatively flat surface on top of the wall has a pretty stand of pillar coral, too.

Orange tube corals and purple tube sponges are just part of the colorful nightlife to be found at Carl's Hill. Photo: G. Lewbel.

Carl's Hill, on the far side of Klein Bonaire, has a profusion of large sponges, such as these purple tubes, growing along the dropoff. Photo: L. Martin.

Giant Sponge. The dropoff to the west is much like the other drop-offs we've described, with one exception: there is a famous purple tube sponge at a depth of about 60 feet (18 meters) a few minutes' swim from the buoy. This sponge was the largest found during the survey of the Bonaire Marine Park.

| **Typical depth range** | : | 20 feet (6 meters) to unlimited |
| **Access** | : | Boat |

Ebo's Reef is on the side of Klein Bonaire that faces Bonaire. There is a narrow shelf inshore of the dropoff which is an ideal spot for photography, especially if you can shoot close-ups. The shelf is honeycombed with short tunnels, caves, elkhorn coral, and fire coral. Lots of fish hide in the tunnels, and it's a great place to spend some time at the end of a deep dive.

The shallow side of Ebo's reef is a wonderland of elkhorn coral in very shallow water. Photo: G. Lewbel.

Black Coral Forests. The dropoff at Ebo's Reef starts at about 20 feet (6 meters). Strictly speaking, the dropoff is not a wall but a very steep slope for much of the distance down to the sand bottom at over 120 (36 meters). The dropoff is not a single slab-like structure, but rather a series of steep buttresses interrupted by wide valleys. The valleys have sand channels in them, and you can probably see sand flowing down them into the depths. The appeal of Ebo's Reef is really the black coral forest, however; the dropoff is famous for black coral. You can see big bushes of it as shallow as 20–30 feet (6–9 meters), just below the crest of the dropoff.

Farther down the slope at Ebo's Reef, the elkhorn gardens give way to giant stands of semi-precious black coral in less than 30 feet (9 meters) of water. Photo: G. Lewbel.

Typical depth range	:	25 feet (8 meters) to unlimited
Access	:	Boat

Something Special is one of the best spots to see garden eels without having to go very deep, and is often visited by tarpon and schools of mullet. It is a dropoff dive, but the slope in most places is quite a bit less than 45°. The buoy is located just south of the entrance to the yacht harbor adjacent to the Hotel Bonaire. When the entrance was cut, a large mound of sand was built up to the south of the breakwater. This sand extends downward from the breakwater and provides a home for many garden eels.

A basket sponge dominates the gradual slope at Something Special, a site just outside the yacht harbor.
Photo: L. Martin.

A large condylactis anemone recoils from the touch of an inquisitive diver. Photo: L. Martin.

To see the dropoff and the garden eels, swim offshore from the mooring buoy; the dropoff begins at about 30 feet (9 meters). As you descend on the slope, keep an eye out for scorpionfish, which are very common here and will cooperate with patient photographers. The dropoff runs into white sand at various depths from 60 feet (18 meters) on down beyond sport diving depths, as the bottom edge of the dropoff also slopes downward to the left (facing seaward). For this reason, set your course from the buoy to take you slightly to the right as you descend, so you hit the sand and the garden eels at about 60 feet (18 meters). If you continue to veer toward the north (left, facing the shore) as you return upslope, your path will bring you back up the strip of sand on the left side (facing shoreward) of the coral-covered dropoff. Stay out of the marina channel, keeping to the outside of the breakwater, and swim up to the sand patch near the base of the breakwater on your way back to the boat. Tarpon and mullet are often seen in this area.

Typical depth range   :   20–120 feet   (5 – 40 meters)
Access   :   Shore

Front Porch is the dive site in front of the Bonaire Scuba Center at the
Hotel Bonaire. The Hotel Bonaire has a fine sandy beach that makes a
perfect entry and exit spot. The shelf in front of the hotel is mainly sand
and is relatively flat and uninteresting, but it is a good place for training
dives or first-time snorkelers. The shelf slopes smoothly down to the edge
of the dropoff at about 20 feet (6 meters). Beyond the edge, the dropoff
continues at about 45° to a white sand bottom at about 120 feet (40
meters).

*A beautiful adult French angel fish is just one of the tame species that can be found off the
beach in front of the Hotel Bonaire. Photo: G. Lewbel.*

The mixed sand and coral bottom at the Front Porch site makes it easier to spot creatures, such as this goldspotted snake eel, that normally hide inside the reef. Photo: G. Lewbel.

The dropoff is not particularly appealing when compared to many others on Bonaire. The area is somewhat sandy, and sponges are more prominent than corals. If you prefer sponges you'll like the spot, but be careful—many of the sponges are of the stinging variety. Most of the coral heads are rather small. On the positive side, there are a lot of fish, and they are so used to divers that they won't mind your popping your strobe in their eyes or trying to take macro shots of their lips. There are also many fish that prefer partial sand cover, such as jawfish and rays. The area is badly littered with trash and broken coral, so please consider carrying back a bit of this trash at the end of your dive to help clean the reef.

La Machaca* 8

Typical depth range	:	20–120 feet (6–36 meters)
Access	:	Shore

In front of Captain Don's Habitat, just seaward of the string of buoys off the pier, is a small wrecked fishing boat, the *La Machaca,* on the bottom at about 35 feet (11 meters). To dive this site, you can enter the water by jumping off the end of the pier in front of the dive shop and exit up the ladder just to the right of the pier (facing land). *La Machaca* is an ideal spot for a night dive, since the pier is well lit during the night and has an easy entrance and exit. Most Habitat customers dive here in the daytime and then return at night.

The *La Machaca* rests upside-down on the edge of a coral-covered dropoff that slopes downward at about 45° and ends on a white sand bottom at about 120 feet (36 meters). The wreck has several big black crinoids that will obligingly pose for you on the hull. There is also a bed of garden eels in the sand at the base of the dropoff.

This incredibly well-developed stand of fire coral can be viewed by divers or snorkelers in the shallow water at La Machacha.

A peacock flounder rests on a coral head near the La Machacha *dropoff, located just in front of the* Habitat. *Photo: L. Martin.*

The dropoff in front of Captain Don's Habitat is the prettiest of the "hotel front" reefs in terms of coral condition (excellent) and trash (nearly none). Hotels tend to generate paper cups, plastic bags, and so on, which sometimes find their way onto the reefs in front of them. Somehow, Habitat has managed to avoid this problem, and seems to have encouraged good buoyancy control and diving habits among the customers because there's much less apparent physical damage to coral on Habitat's reef. The reef is in near-perfect shape.

On either side of the Habitat pier you'll find some big heads of elkhorn coral and staghorn coral in 10–20 feet (3–6 meters) of water. Look for the fluffy nudibranchs ("lettuce slugs") in the staghorn thickets. To the right of the pier (facing seaward), well-covered snorkelers and divers will enjoy seeing a beautiful bed of fire coral.

Typical depth range	:	30 feet (9 meters) to unlimited
Access	:	Boat or shore

Cliff has one of the relatively few vertical walls you'll find on Bonaire. It's a good site for intermediates because it's fairly shallow and may be considered a brief, steep section in a gradual dropoff. The wall begins at about 30 feet (9 meters), drops straight down to about 60–70 feet (18–21 meters), and then slopes at about 45° to below sport diving depths. Cliff makes a good training spot for divers who have not had a lot of wall experience, since you'll be stopped by the slope if you descend to the base of the wall.

Corals. The wall has lots of wire coral and quite a bit of black coral, too. You can find big sheet corals on the lower parts of the wall, lots of fish, layers of star coral, and quite a few moray eels in nooks and crannies.

The easiest way to dive Cliff from the shore is to jump off the pier at Habitat and swim along the shelf to the first Park buoy north of the pier. It's about a ten-minute swim, and the shelf near shore is covered with fire coral as well as elkhorn and staghorn coral. The shelf north of Habitat is perfect for snorkelers, too.

A spotted moray eel hides beneath a small cap of star coral at The Cliff. Photo: L. Martin.

Typical depth range	:	30 feet (9 meters) to unlimited
Access	:	Boat or shore

Ol' Blue is located just two buoys south of the Karpata Ecological Center. It has a narrow shelf and a dropoff less than five minutes' swim from a beach covered with coral rubble. The lip of the dropoff is about 30 feet (9 meters) deep, and the dropoff slopes downward gently to a depth of about 60 feet (18 meters), then crests again, and descends more steeply until it flattens out beyond 120 feet (36 meters).

Fantastic Corals and Sponges. Ol' Blue is well-known for its monster finger sponges. Take your wide-angle lens to this spot. There are several "nests" of purple sponges with branches more than 10 feet (3 meters) long, entangled together and looking like spaghetti sticking up into the water. Most of the sponges are in the 60–80 foot (18–25 meter) depth range. Ol' Blue also has some unusual sheet coral near the base of the dropoff, forming mounds similar to stacks of dishes.

A profusion of coral species and a Spanish hogfish greet divers at the dropoff at The Cliff. Photo: L. Martin.

Typical depth range	:	30 feet (9 meters) to unlimited
Access	:	Boat or shore

Karpata is an old favorite with local divers and a first choice for many visiting divers. Karpata is the most northerly dive site outside Washington/Slagbaai National Park. Across the road from the steps leading down to the beach is the Karpata Ecological Center, the headquarters of the Netherlands Antilles National Parks Foundation that administers the Bonaire Marine Park. Although there are few exhibits at the Center, visitors are usually welcome.

Karpata is exposed sometimes to wave action, and the terrace near shore has lots of broken coral. The edge of the wall is within five minute's swim offshore and crests at about 30–40 feet (9–12 meters). The crest has several extremely interesting features. If you go along the crest to the left of the steps on the beach (facing seaward), you can find a huge old anchor—the old-fashioned sailor's tattoo kind—embedded right in the lip of the wall at about 35 feet (11 meters). There are also some gigantic sea fans near the crest. Some of them are so large that two divers can hide behind them.

Spanish hogfish, such as this beautiful specimen, are often lacking in shallow waters of Caribbean islands due to overfishing. The marine park status of shallow areas of Bonaire has made the area a haven for hogfish. Photo: G. Lewbel.

Trumpetfish are often seen as they try to hide within or against a formation of soft coral. Photo: H. Taylor.

Over the crest from the anchor is a near-vertical wall that drops to well below 100 feet (30 meters) before beginning to level off. The wall is interrupted by beautiful canyons formed by large buttresses. An excellent scenic tour would take you down over the lip at the anchor, along the wall toward the west, back up one of the canyons to the lip, and then up onto the shelf again.

Typical depth range	:	40–100 feet (12–30 meters)
Access	:	Shore

Boca Bartól is at the northern end of Bonaire Island, in Washington/ Slagbaai Park. It is exposed to wave action and often has heavy surf and currents. If you are not a very experienced diver with training in surf entries and exits, read no further—this dive is not for you. Even if you have the necessary skills, I recommend that you dive Boca Bartól only on calm days and only with a qualified guide who is familiar with the area. Boca Bartól can change from calm to rough on short notice. The easiest entrance and exit is the small beach at the southern edge of the cove (to your left as you face the sea), but you can still get thrown around by surf at this beach, even on fairly calm days.

Deep Sea Canyons. Boca Bartól is a large open cove that is deeply furrowed with ridges of corals that biologists call spur-and-groove formations. The cove has a sandy bottom, and long parallel ridges run from near shore out to the edge of the dropoff. Swimming across the tops of these spurs is like flying an airplane over rows of steep canyons. Most of the ridges are about 20 feet (6 meters) high, rising out of a sand bottom about 30 feet (19 meters) deep. Between the ridges you can expect to see many groupers, Peacock flounders, large sting rays, midnight parrotfish, and other big fish.

The seaward edges of the ridges are about 10 minutes' swim from the beach under calm conditions. If there's any current running, I suggest that you not continue farther offshore but return to the beach between the ridges. If there is no current, the dropoff is worth the additional 10 minutes' swim to see. The sand continues out from the spurs to the dropoff. The edge of the dropoff begins at various depths depending on the location, but is 60 feet (18 meters) or deeper in most places. The dropoff has coral mounds interspersed with sand waterfalls that continue down the slope into very deep water.

Two large condylactis anemones share a coral head at Boca Bartol. Their color, as seen in these two, ranges from light sea green to delicate shade of lavender. Photo: G. Lewbel. ▶

Typical depth range   :   40 feet (12 meters) to unlimited
Access   :   Beach

The best diving in this area is south of the huts, but plan your dive so that you swim north into the current, which can be strong at times. Once at the dropoff (about 300 feet or 90 meters from shore), you can expect to see large gorgonians thriving in the current and a large variety of sponges. Big fish can generally be seen here too. Large groupers, snappers, and parrotfish are seen here frequently and stingrays and turtles are not uncommon sights.

The beach here is broken coral rubble, which makes for difficult walking especially when loaded with equipment. Diving from a boat makes for clean, easy entries and exits.

A large solitary coral polyp nestles in among scattered brain coral and star coral colonies. Photo: G. Lewbel.

A boulder of mountainous star coral and large stand of purple tube sponges front the dropoff just offshore from the slave huts. Photo: G. Lewbel.

Lost War Ship

The *HMS Barhem,* a British Man-of-War, went aground in this area on April 29, 1829. It had 74 cannons on board, 37 of which were thrown overboard in an attempt to refloat the stranded ship. Only a few of the Scottish-made cannons have been recovered to date, so there is a good chance to see more underwater. If you miss them, you can see some of the recovered cannons in front of the Bonaire Trading Company and in front of the Dutch World Broadcasting System building.

Willemstoren Lighthouse 14

Typical depth range	:	40–60 feet (12–18 meters)
Access	:	Beach

This dive can almost be classified as a windward-side dive. It is at the southernmost point of the island, where the line between the windward and leeward sides is drawn. It can be an excellent dive, but you must be a strong swimmer and know how to make an entry through the surf, which is usually present. The idea is to get under the surf and out to the deeper water as quickly as possible. On exiting, you should swim into shallow water as far as you can, stand and remove your fins, and then walk out of the surf quickly. Plan your dive so that you can swim southwest (to the

The lighthouse at Willemstoren has been warning ships away from this coral point since 1838. Photo: H. Taylor.

Many large anchors are found off Willemstoren. Before the lighthouse was constructed ships often went up on the reef here. Photo: G. Lewbel.

right when facing the ocean); this way you will be swimming against the current. Avoid being caught in the current at this point because the next land mass is too far to swim.

Great sea fans waving back and forth in the current will probably be the first thing you notice here. At the dropoff, coral growth is dense and quite lush. The marine life here tends to be larger than on the other leeward sites of the island and there is a good chance to see sea turtles here. Anchors and chains are frequently seen in this area because many wrecks have been lost on this corner of the island. Until 1762, the point was unmarked at night, and then only with bonfires. The first permanent lighthouse was built in 1838.

5

Diving in Aruba

Although less known for underwater sports than its famous sister, Bonaire, and even less than Curacao, Aruba is gaining a reputation among couples where just one partner dives. Elegant topside accommodations, glittering casinos, shopping and nightlife are enough to sate the most commercial minded.

Underwater, several wrecks to the west and patch reefs and a wall around the southern tip of the island offer the usual amenities of the Caribbean—colorful sponges, lush coral growth and brilliant marine life. The portions may be a bit smaller than you'll find around Bonaire, but if you're interested in a more lively resort life, the trade may be a good one.

Diving services on Aruba are more oriented to the casual diver than the bottom-time junkie. Packages are available with accommodations at the generally expensive luxury resorts or at more economical deluxe hotels. Most offer two tank dives daily, although half-day two tank dives, full-day three tank dives and night dives are also available.

Queen angelfish are frequently seen at many sites in the Antilles, often in pairs. Photo: H. Taylor.

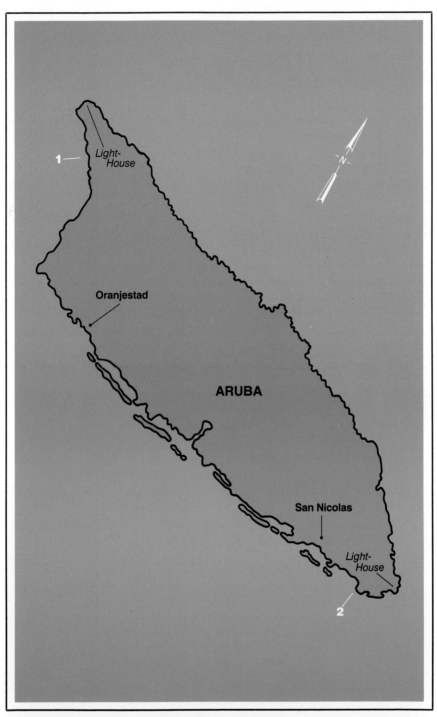

In terms of diving Aruba has been the step-sister of the ABCs. With a firm reputation for night life, it's now adding scuba to its list of aquatic attractions.

Antilla 1

Typical depth range	:	60 feet (18 meters)
Access	:	Boat

The *Antilla* was a German freighter which was lying off Aruba when World War II broke out in Europe. The crew scuttled the vessel to prevent her being captured.

The central mast of the steel craft breaks the surface, a big crossbar breaking up the swells that lap at the spar.

The *Antilla* broke in two parts when she went down, and although the wreck has attracted the attention of at least two generations of divers, it is, in a sense, a virgin find. Many of the interior compartments have never been opened or explored.

The steelwork extending up from the main deck towards the surface is dizzying. Having been down more than 40 years, the rusting metal is well coated with a sheath of living marine growth. Halfway up the mast, a colony of orange tube sponges branches off like a bunch of ripe undersea bananas. Red encrusting sponge and colonies of delicate orange tube coral crowd basket sponges of various hues for a footing on the steel rigging.

Like most wrecks, the *Antilla* has attracted its share of fish. Schools of yellowtails cruise the site, wandering back and forth from one section to the other. Smaller species hide in the nooks and crannies afforded by the prolific sponge and coral growth.

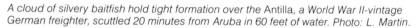

A cloud of silvery baitfish hold tight formation over the Antilla, *a World War II-vintage German freighter, scuttled 20 minutes from Aruba in 60 feet of water. Photo: L. Martin.*

Orange coral can be seen at many dive sites . Photo: H. Taylor.

South Wall

Typical depth range   :   10–100 feet
Access   :   Boat

The south end of Aruba offers a variety of dive sites and settings. Shallow patch reefs, typical of the Antilles, are found reasonably close to shore, and they're good fare for snorkeling excursions for the uncertified.

   While the close-in reefs, in particular, don't have the pristine clarity of Bonaire's near-shore coral gardens, visibility on the wall is commonly 100 plus feet (more than 30 meters).

   The lip of the wall is somewhat deeper here than on Bonaire, with some portions starting at about 50 feet (18 meters). Due to the casual nature of the scuba arrangements, boat operators generally prefer to reserve wall diving for the more experienced.

Plate coral, sometimes called lettuce coral or scroll coral, hangs from the south wall. Photo: L. Martin.

Although the south wall starts a little deeper than some of the dropoff areas around Bonaire, the sights can be worth the extra depth. A bonus is that all of this is a short boat trip from international-class restaurants, hotels and nightclubs. Photo: S. Blount.

6

Safety

This chapter discusses common hazards and emergency procedures in case of a diving accident. It does not discuss the diagnosis or treatment of serious medical problems; refer to your first aid manual or emergency diving manual for that information.

DAN. The Divers Alert Network (DAN), a membership association of individuals and organizations sharing a common interest in diving safety operates a **24 hour national hotline (919) 684-8111** (collect calls are accepted in an emergency). DAN does not directly provide medical care, however they do provide advice on early treatment, evacuation and hyperbaric treatment of diving related injuries. Additionally, DAN provides diving safety information to members to help prevent accidents. Membership is $10 a year, offering: the DAN *Underwater Diving Accident Manual,* describing symptoms and first aid for the major diving related injuries, emergency room physician guidelines for drugs and i.v. fluids; a membership card listing diving related symptoms on one side and DAN's emergency and non emergency phone numbers on the other; 1 tank decal and 3 small equipment decals with DAN's logo and emergency number; and a newsletter, "Alert Diver" describes diving medicine and safety information in layman's language with articles for professionals, case histories, and medical questions related to diving. Special membership for dive stores, dive clubs, and corporations are also available. The DAN manual can be purchased for $4 from the Administrative Coordinator, National Diving Alert Network, Duke University Medical Center, Box 3823, Durham, NC 27710.

DAN divides the U.S. into 7 regions, each coordinated by a specialist in diving medicine who has access to the skilled hyperbaric chambers in his region. Non emergency or information calls are connected to the DAN office and information number, (919) 684-2948. This number can be dialed direct, between 9 a.m. and 5 p.m. Monday-Friday Eastern Standard time. Chamber status can change frequently making this kind of information dangerous if obsolete at the time of an emergency. Instead, divers should contact DAN as soon as a diving emergency is suspected. All divers should have comprehensive medical insurance and check to make sure that hyperbaric treatment and air ambulance services are covered internationally.

Diving is a safe sport and there are very few accidents compared to the number of divers and number of dives made each year. But when the infrequent injury does occur, DAN is ready to help. DAN, originally 100% federally funded, is now largely supported by the diving public. Membership in DAN or purchase of DAN manuals or decals provides divers with useful safety information and provides DAN with necessary operating funds. Donations to DAN are tax deductible as DAN is a legal non-profit public service organization.

I have suggested some ways to contact medical personnel as rapidly as possible. The telephone numbers and addresses given in this edition were current to the best of the author's knowledge in early 1984, but the author assumes no responsibility for assuring that phone numbers or contact information are correct. Emergency contact information can change so check on it during or just before the time of your dive trip.

In case of a diving accident, such as a lung injury or decompression sickness ("bends"), prompt recompression treatment in a chamber may be essential to prevent permanent injury or death. There is a four-person, double-lock recompression chamber at the St. Elisabeth Hospital (St. Elisabeth Gasthuis) on the Punda side of downtown Willemstad in Curacao. The hospital is located between J.H.J. Hamelbergweg, Breedestraat, and Pater Eeuwensweg; telephone 24900 or 25100. The chamber is staffed by a group of very well-qualified cardiac and pulmonary specialists, and has an ample supply of oxygen and compressed air.

If you're injured on Bonaire you'll need to get over to Curacao, but this is not as difficult as it sounds. There is a large network of private pilots in the Netherlands Antilles, and they and ALM Antillean Airlines work together to evacuate patients to Curacao. The fastest way to handle the evacuation is probably to notify any one of the divemasters (such as Dave Serlin at Captain Don's Habitat, phone 8290, or Craig Burns at Dive Bonaire at the Flamingo Beach, phone 8285) and ask for help.

If you need recompression while in the Netherlands Antilles, I recommend that you get it there rather than attempt to fly to the chambers in the States. Should there be a need for emergency assistance after leaving the Netherlands Antilles—and remember, bends symptoms sometimes don't show up for many hours after a dive, and are sometimes brought on by flying—we recommend that you contact DAN immediately.

Hazardous Marine Animals

Sea Urchins. As in the rest of the Caribbean, the most common hazardous animal that divers will encounter in the Netherlands Antilles is the long-spined sea urchin. In fact, the species name reflects its home here: the urchin's scientific name is *Diadema antillarum*, meaning diadem or crown of the Antilles. This urchin has spines that can penetrate wetsuits, booties, and gloves. Injuries are nearly always immediately painful, and sometimes infect. Urchins are found at every diving depth, although they are more common in shallow water near shore, especially under coral heads. At night the urchins come out of their hiding places and are even easier to bump into. Minor injuries can be treated by extracting the spines (it's worth a try, though they're hard to get out) and treating the wound with antibiotic cream; make sure your tetanus immunization is current. Usually, spine bits fester and pop out several weeks later. Some people feel that crushing an embedded spine (ouch!) will make it dissolve faster in the tissues. Serious punctures will require a doctor's attention.

Fire Coral. Fire coral is most common in shallow water along the terraces above dropoffs, but can grow as an encrusting form on dead gorgonians or coral at any depth. Contact with fire coral causes a burning feeling which usually goes away in a minute or two. In some individuals, contact results in red welts. Cortisone cream can reduce the inflammation.

A member of the family of scorpion fishes, stone fish lie almost hidden among clumps of coral and rock. Spines along their dorsal fins can inject a powerful poison if they're brushed or stepped on. Photo: G. Lewbel.

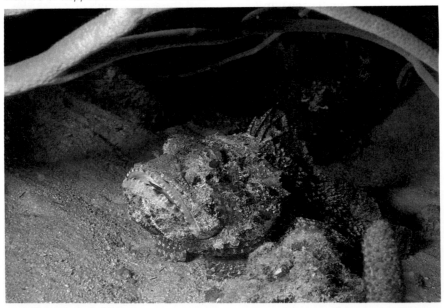

Coral cuts and scrapes also can irritate and frequently infect. Minor coral scratches can be treated successfully with antibiotic cream, but serious cuts should be handled by a doctor, especially if broken bits of coral are embedded in the wound.

Bristle Worms. Fire worms (also called bristle worms) can be found on most reefs. If you touch one, it will embed tiny stinging bristles in your skin and cause a burning sensation that may be followed by the development of a red spot or welt. The sensation is similar to touching fire coral or one of those fuzzy soft-looking cactuses on land. The bristles will eventually work their way out of your skin in a couple of days. You can try to scrape them off with the edge of a sharp knife or pull them off with adhesive tape. Cortisone cream helps reduce local inflammation.

Sponges. Sponges also have fine spicules, and some species have a chemical irritant that is immediately painful. You'll be pleased to know that the species name of one of the worst, *Neofibularia nolitangere*, means "do not touch." Although their bright red color is sometimes a clue to the bad ones, it's not completely reliable. I have been stung by various innocuous-looking sponges. If you get spicules in your skin, you can try the same tricks I suggested for fire worms, or douse the skin with mild vinegar or mild ammonia (this sometimes works, sometimes not). The stinging sensation usually goes away within a day, and cortisone cream helps.

Sting Rays. Sting rays can be seen in sand flats. There are two Caribbean species: the southern sting ray (very large, diamond-shaped, and difficult to approach) and the yellow sting ray (small, shaped like a hubcap, and easy to approach). The southern sting ray seems more common around Bonaire and Curacao. Neither will attack, but they don't like being sat on, stepped on, or prodded. They often are partially covered with sand, so look before you settle down on sandy bottoms. The long barbed stinger at the base of the tail can inflict a serious wound. Wounds are always extremely painful, often deep and infective, and can cause serious symptoms including anaphylactic shock. If you get stung, head for the hospital and let a doctor take care of the wound.

Stonefish. Scorpionfishes, or stone fishes, are quite common in the Netherlands Antilles. They are well camouflaged, usually less than a foot (30 centimeters) long, and have poisonous spines hidden among their fins. They are often difficult to spot because they typically sit quietly on the bottom, looking more like plant-covered rocks than live fish. As with sting rays, watch where you put your hands and knees and you're not likely to meet one the hard way. If you get stung, severe allergic reactions are quite possible and great pain and infection are virtually certain, so head for the hospital and see a doctor.

Eels. Moray eels are dangerous only if harassed. There are lots of morays under coral heads and in crevices, and cornered eels will bite. On Bonaire and Klein Bonaire, dive guides have been hand-feeding morays for quite some time at selected sites.

Sharks. Sharks are not common at any of the sites mentioned in this book. It would be a rare occurrence to see a shark once out of hundreds of dives, but if you do see one, it will probably be a nurse shark sleeping under a ledge. Don't worry—they eat shellfish, not divers—but don't hassle them because they wake up grumpy and have bitten a number of divers in other locations. Any shark injury calls for immediate medical attention, obviously.

Barracudas. Barracudas are included in this section only because of their undeserved reputation for ferocity. You'll be lucky to get one close enough for a good photograph. They're rather timid about coming closer than a few yards. At night, you can sometimes get within touching distance of a sleeping barracuda.

Sea Wasps: A Hazard for Night Divers. Speaking of night diving, do avoid sea wasps! Sea wasps are small jellyfish, usually less than 6 inches (15 centimeters) long, that pack a tremendous wallop in their tentacles. Sea wasps are transparent and shaped like an elongated cube (hence the family name, *Cubomedusae*). They have four stubby tentacles. They live in very deep water during the day but swim to the surface at night to feed. They are apparently attracted to lights and gather just below the surface, where they catch other invertebrates and fish. To reduce your chances of getting stung on a night dive, wear gloves and a full wetsuit or other protection, don't snorkel or linger near the surface, and look for sea wasps before you jump into the water or make your ascent.

A purplemouth eel displays the usual, open-jawed posture. Eels open and close their mouths to pump water over their gills, not to threaten divers. Their teeth are sharp and strong, however, and wise divers usually steer clear of the defensive animals.
Photo: G. Lewbel.

Appendix 1: Dive Shops

Curacao

Dive Curacao/Princess Beach Hotel
Hotel Travel Resources
501 Madison Avenue
New York, NY 10022
212 935-9279

Masterdive Scubashop
Fokkerweg 13
Willemstad, Curacao, N.A.
54312

Subseas Curacao
Grenadaweg 10
80271

Piscadera Watersports
Curacao Concord Hotel
25000 ext. 177 or
25905

Bonaire

Bonaire Scuba Center/ Bonaire
  Beach Hotel
Bonaire Tours Inc.
U.S. Sales and Reservations
100 Parker Street
Morgan, NJ 08879
201 566-8866
outside NJ: 800 526-2370

Bachelor's Beach Apartments,
Bonaire Beach Bungalows,
Carib Inn, and
Sunset Villas
c/o Bonaire Vacations Ltd.
580 Plandome Road
Manhasset, NY 11030
800 622-2742

Captain Don's Habitat
Frank Fennell, Aquaventure
International
P.O. Box 237,
Waitsfield, VT 05673

Dive Bonaire/Flamingo Beach Hotel
P.O. Box 686
Ithaca, NY 14850
800 847-7198
In NY: 800 252-6323

Carabala Bungalows
Buddy Watersports N.V.
P.O. Box 95
Bonaire, Netherland Antilles
599-7-8065 or 8365

Aruba

Aruba Tourist Bureau
A. Shuttestraat 2
Oranjestad, Aruba
23777

Aruba Tourist Bureau
1270 Avenue of the Americas
Suite 2212
New York, NY 10020
212 246-3030

Aruba Tourist Bureau
399 N.E. 15th St.
Miami, FL 33132
305 358-6360

De Palm Tours
L.G. Smith Boulevard 142
P.O. Box 656
Oranjestad, Aruba N.A.
24400-24545

Index